by Kevin Blake

Consultant: Marjorie Faulstich Orellana, PhD
Professor of Urban Schooling
University of California, Los Angeles

BEARPORT
PUBLISHING

New York, New York

Credits

Cover, © Mahathir Mohd Yasin/Shutterstock and © Pelikh Alexey/Shutterstock; TOC, © sommai damrongpanich/Shutterstock; 4, © Boule/Shutterstock; 5T, © ESB Professional/Shutterstock; 5B, © fazon1/iStock; 7, © Adel Newman/Shutterstock; 8L, © Mazur Travel/Shutterstock; 8–9, © THPStock/Shutterstock; 9R, © CRStudio/Shutterstock; 10, © Oulailax Nakhone/Shutterstock; 11T, © Viktar Malyshchyts/Shutterstock; 11B, © Hasnuddin/Shutterstock; 12T, © Photocech/iStock; 12B, © Skynavin/Shutterstock; 13T, © Jacus/iStock; 13B, © TigerStock's/Shutterstock; 14, © Dorling Kindersley ltd/Alamy; 15, © Pictures from History/David Henley/Bridgeman Images; 16, © Pictures from History/Bridgeman Images; 17T, © Lano Lan/Shutterstock; 17B, © Hafiz Johari/Shutterstock; 18–19, © ESB Professional/Shutterstock; 20, © iyd39/Shutterstock; 21, © yongyuan/iStock; 22L, © Nitikom Poonsiri/Shutterstock; 22–23, © dolphfyn/Shutterstock; 24–25, © Sirisak_baokaew/Shutterstock; 25R, © photobykierara96/Shutterstock; 26, © joharhu/Shutterstock; 27, © abdul hafiz ab hamid/Shutterstock; 28, © Hafizussalam bin Sulaiman/Shutterstock; 29, © BartCo/iStock; 30T, © melisamok/Shutterstock, © Fat Jackey/Shutterstock, and © Elena Odareeva/Shutterstock; 30B, © ThamKC/Shutterstock; 31 (T to B), © Patrick Foto/Shutterstock, Public Domain, © michel arnault/Shutterstock, © Khai9000Pictures/Shutterstock, © ixpert/Shutterstock, and © Yatra/Shutterstock; 32, © spatuletail/Shutterstock.

Publisher: Kenn Goin
Senior Editor: Joyce Tavolacci
Creative Director: Spencer Brinker
Design: Debrah Kaiser
Photo Researcher: Thomas Persano

Library of Congress Cataloging-in-Publication Data

Names: Blake, Kevin, 1978– author.
Title: Malaysia / by Kevin Blake.
Description: New York, New York : Bearport Publishing, 2020. | Series:
  Countries we come from | Includes bibliographical references and index.
Identifiers: LCCN 2019007136 (print) | LCCN 2019008304 (ebook) | ISBN
  9781642805895 (ebook) | ISBN 9781642805352 (library)
Subjects: LCSH: Malaysia—Juvenile literature.
Classification: LCC DS592 (ebook) | LCC DS592 .B67 2020 (print) | DDC
  959.5—dc23
LC record available at https://lccn.loc.gov/2019007136

For more information, write to Bearport Publishing Company, Inc., 45 West 21st Street, Suite 3B, New York, New York 10010. Printed in the United States of America.

10 9 8 7 6 5 4 3 2 1

Contents

Colorful

ANCIENT

BUSY

Malaysia (muh-LAY-zhuh) is a country in Southeast Asia.

Half of Malaysia is on a **peninsula**. The other half is on an island.

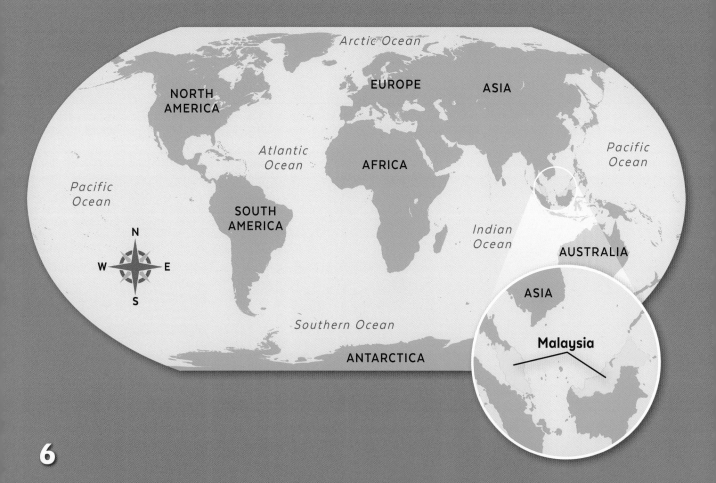

About 32 million people live in Malaysia.

Malaysia has thick rain forests. Long rivers wind across the land.

Malaysian forests are home to rafflesias (ruh-FLEE-zhuz). These plants have the world's heaviest flowers!

Powerful storms called monsoons (mon-SOONS) bring lots of rain.

Because of all the rain, Malaysia's land is very **fertile**.

rice plants

Farmers grow rice in wet fields.

Farmers also grow bananas, mangoes, and pineapples.

pineapples

Malaysia has most of the world's rubber trees. The trees' **sap** is used to make rubber bands and tires!

11

There's incredible wildlife in Malaysia!

There are tigers in the forests.

King cobras slither across the ground.

Giant elephants feed on plants.

The rhinoceros hornbill has a huge beak. It's the national bird of Malaysia.

Malaysia has a long history.

People settled there 10,000 years ago!

They hunted, fished, and farmed.

Then, Europeans arrived in the 1500s. Soon after, they took control of the land.

The Portuguese and Dutch controlled Malaysia for hundreds of years.

15

In the 1800s, Malaysia became a British **colony**.

The British cut down forests and planted rubber trees.

They brought people from India and China to work on the farms.

British colonialists in Malaysia

The workers were treated badly by the British.

British rule finally ended in 1957.

On August 31, 1957, Malaysia became a free country.

Today, a king rules Malaysia.

Sultan Abdullah of Pahang

The **capital** of Malaysia is Kuala Lumpur (KWAH-luh lum-POOR).

It's also the country's largest city.

It has some of the tallest buildings in the world!

Petronas Towers

The Petronas Towers are 1,483 feet (452 m)—or 88 stories—tall!

19

Malaysia's main language is Malay.

This is how you say *good day* in Malay:

Selamat siang
(suh-la-MAT SEE-ang)

This is how you say *tiger*:

Harimau
(har-ee-MAO)

Many people in
Malaysia also
speak English.

Malaysian food is flavorful.

Many dishes include creamy coconut milk.

Hot chilies add spice to food.

Rice is eaten with most meals.

Teh tarik—a kind of hot tea—is a popular drink.

What sports do Malaysians play?

People enjoy soccer!

Malaysians also love badminton.

It's played with rackets and a shuttlecock.

shuttlecock

Malaysians practice *silat* (sih-LAT). It's a kind of a **martial art**.

25

Malaysia is known for beautiful batik (buh-TEEK) fabric.

To make batik, people use wax to create patterns on cloth.

Then, they dye the cloth bright colors.

Malaysians often wear batik on important days.

Look up in the sky!
Malaysians fly huge
kites called *wau bulan*
(WOW bah-LAN).

The big kites are made from paper.
They make whirring sounds when they fly!

Farmers once used wau bulan to scare away birds from their fields.

29

Fast Facts

Capital city:
Kuala Lumpur

Population of Malaysia:
About 32 million

Main language:
Malay

Money: Ringgit

Major religion: Islam

Neighboring countries:
Brunei, Indonesia, and Thailand

Cool Fact: Malaysia is home to a cave with a huge room inside. It's called the Sarawak Chamber. This special cave room is the largest ever found!

capital (KAP-uh-tuhl) the city where a country's government is based

colony (KOL-uh-nee) a country controlled by another country, usually a distant one

fertile (fur-TUHL) rich, or capable of producing lots of crops

martial art (MAR-shuhl ART) a style of fighting for self-defense

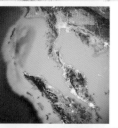

peninsula (puh-NIN-soo-la) land surrounded by water on three sides

sap (SAP) a liquid that carries water and nutrients through a plant

Index

Read More

Bankston, John. *We Visit Malaysia (Your Land and My Land: Asia).* Hockessin, DE: Mitchell Lane (2014).

Owings, Lisa. *Malaysia (Exploring Countries).* Minneapolis, MN: Bellwether (2014).

Learn More Online

To learn more about Malaysia, visit
www.bearportpublishing.com/CountriesWeComeFrom

About the Author

Kevin Blake lives in Providence, Rhode Island, with his wife, Melissa, his son, Sam, and his daughter, Ilana. He'd love to take a trip to Malaysia soon!